An Industry Intelligence Report from CEG Worldwide

In Partnership with **Meridian-IQ**

At the Leading Edge

What a Select Group of Young Financial Advisors Can Teach the Industry

John J. Bowen Jr.
Paul Brunswick
Jonathan J. Powell

At the Leading Edge: What a Select Group of Young Financial Advisors Can Teach the Industry
By John J. Bowen Jr., Paul Brunswick and Jonathan J. Powell

CEG Worldwide, LLC • 1954 Hayes Lane • San Martin, CA 95046 • (888) 551-3824
www.cegworldwide.com • info@cegworldwide.com

Table of Contents

Introduction

Video Overview: www.cegworldwide.com/lead

IN OUR HIGHLY COMPETITIVE INDUSTRY THAT OFFERS financial advisors the opportunity to make a tremendous impact for their clients, team members and families, many are in constant pursuit of the answer to a single question: What drives success?

No two people would answer this question the same way, but most of us would cite a mix of many factors, including our circumstances, ambition, experience, education, natural talent, the choices we have made and that mysterious thing called luck.

Over the past decade, we have carried out this mission by conducting extensive industry research and then disseminating the results of that work through our in-depth coaching programs, hundreds of articles, dozens of webinars, several books and many reports such as the one you have in your hands right now.

More often than not, we have measured the success of financial advisors with one easily understood standard: net income. It was no different when we published *The Client-Centric Shift* in 2012. That report, which was drawn from a nationwide study of more than 2,100 financial advisors, focused on the approaches of those earning net incomes of $500,000 or more a year. As with much of our previous research, we found that the top-income financial advisors often leverage best practices that others do not.

We also found that there is frequently—but certainly not always—a correlation between financial advisors' years of experience and their incomes. This suggests that for many, simply remaining in business and paying one's dues will in time lead to greater financial rewards.

But the data revealed something else: a small number of financial advisors who had completely bucked this trend. These financial advisors were quite new to the industry—all with less than five years of experience—but were already managing more assets than many advisors with far more experience. In fact, they had already reached a milestone in assets under management—$50 million—that many financial advisors never achieve in their entire careers.

Intrigued, we decided to dig deeper to understand how these financial advisors had launched themselves to the top ranks of their profession in such a short time. Our goal was to uncover their clues for success and make this information available to all financial advisors interested in moving to a higher level of success as well as to senior executives looking for insight on hiring the financial advisors who will quickly achieve success. *At the Leading Edge* contains the results of our investigation into this select group.

We rely throughout on data collected during an August 2012 online survey in which we contacted more than 380,000 financial advisors nationwide.

EXHIBIT 1
The Four Quadrants

		Years Practiced	
		Less than five	*More than five*
AUM	*Less than $50 million*	Newcomers	Rank and File
	More than $50 million	Quick Starters	The Elite

Source: CEG Worldwide, 2012.

Exhibit 1 illustrates how we analyzed our survey data according to respondents' assets under management and number of years working as financial advisors, while **Exhibit 2** shows the distribution of the study group.

EXHIBIT 2
The Study Group

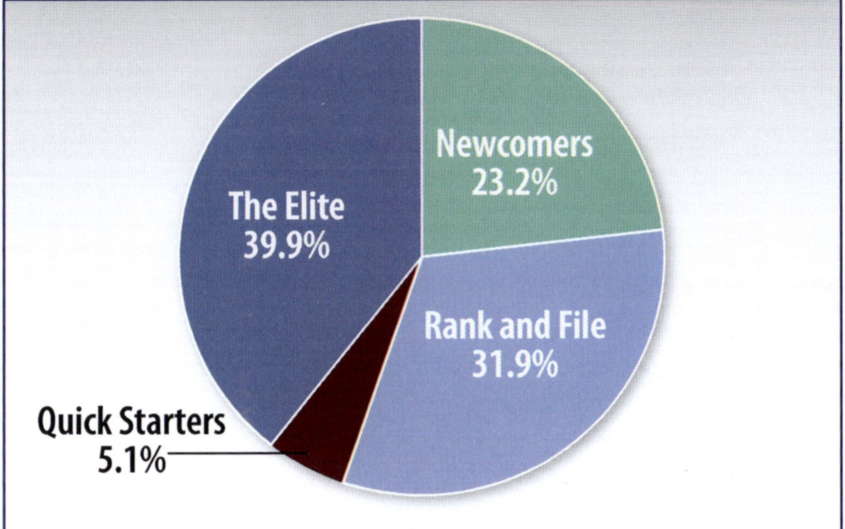

N = 2,128 financial advisors. Source: CEG Worldwide, 2012.

As you can see from the exhibits, there are four quadrants:

- **Newcomers:** These financial advisors are new to the industry, having practiced for less than five years, and manage less than $50 million in assets. They make up slightly less than one-quarter (23.2 percent) of the advisors we surveyed.
- **Rank and File:** Comprising just under one-third of surveyed advisors (31.9 percent), the Rank and File are industry veterans but have not yet hit the $50 million mark in assets under management.

- **Quick Starters:** Like the Newcomers, the Quick Starters have been practicing for less than five years. Unlike the Newcomers, they are already experiencing substantial success, with each managing at least $50 million in assets. Although this group is small—just 5.1 percent of the respondents—we believe there is much to learn from it.
- **The Elite:** Two out of five (39.9 percent) are financial advisors who are well-established in their practices, with at least five years under their belts, and who are managing a minimum of $50 million in assets.

Our focus throughout this report will be on the Quick Starters—where they are similar to financial advisors in the other groups and, more important, where they differ.

But we will do more than simply paint a picture of these young standouts. Our intent is also to help you implement the actions that have put them on the fast track. To that end, we will provide specific steps for applying each action in your own practice. Nearly all of these recommendations have been rigorously tested by the elite financial advisors who take part in our coaching programs, and all of them have been shown to deliver results, again and again.

To set the stage, we will start with an overview of the financial advisors from all four quadrants. From there, we will delve into each of the four major strategies we see the most successful financial advisors using to make the biggest gains:

1. Designing the practice to add the greatest value for select clients
2. Implementing processes to serve clients extremely well
3. Leveraging specific techniques to effectively acquire new clients and assets
4. Engaging in focused planning in order to purposefully grow the business

The Four Quadrants: A Portrait of Today's Financial Advisors

Video Overview: www.cegworldwide.com/lead1

IN THIS INITIAL SECTION, WE WILL OUTLINE THE KEY characteristics of each of the four quadrants of financial advisors today. Some are demographic characteristics, such as age and gender, but most clearly point to decisions that advisors have made about how they serve their clients and manage their practices. This will give us a baseline understanding of the fundamentally different approaches taken by financial advisors in each quadrant.

Age and Gender

In analyzing our data, two things about the Quick Starters struck us immediately. First, they are overwhelmingly young. As **Exhibit 3** shows, four out of five, or 79.6 percent, are 34 years of age or younger. Given that the Quick Starters have been practicing for less than five years, it is not surprising that this is a younger group than both the Rank and File and The Elite. What is surprising is just how much younger this group is—younger, even, than the Newcomers, who manage fewer assets.

Given their ages, we surmise that the financial services industry is a first career for most Quick Starters. These are largely not seasoned professionals who have switched midlife from other occupations.

Second, women are represented more strongly in the Quick Starter group than in the other three groups. (See **Exhibit 4.**) Of the financial advisors we surveyed, 18.1 percent were women (reflecting the degree to which women are statistically underrepresented in the industry). Among the

EXHIBIT 3
Ages of Financial Advisors in the Four Quadrants

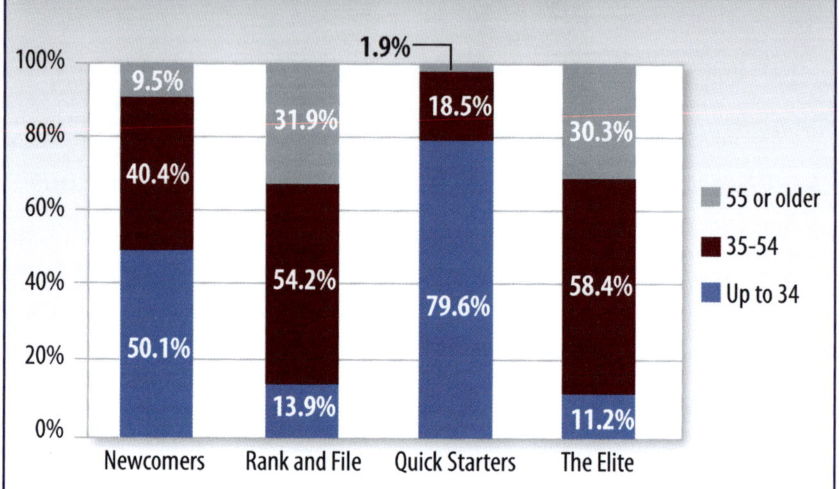

N = 2,123 financial advisors. Source: CEG Worldwide, 2012.

Quick Starters, that number was much higher: 31.4 percent. Because women make up far less of the Newcomer group (20.8 percent), we cannot attribute the higher percentage of female Quick Starters simply to greater representation of women in younger cohorts in the industry—if that were the case, we would expect both the Quick Starter and Newcomer groups to represent women more heavily than the other groups.

What do we make of these data on age and gender? Clearly, simply being young or being a woman does not make one more likely to acquire significant assets to manage. But perhaps being new to their industry or being part of a group that continues to be underrepresented in the industry—or both—enables these financial advisors to approach their work with greater openness to more possibilities. Not burdened by legacy business issues and with fewer preconceptions of how they "should" operate their practices and serve their clients, they are freer to pursue new and perhaps more effective approaches. This flexibility and dexterity is particularly valuable in today's rapidly shifting environment.

EXHIBIT 4
Women in the Four Quadrants

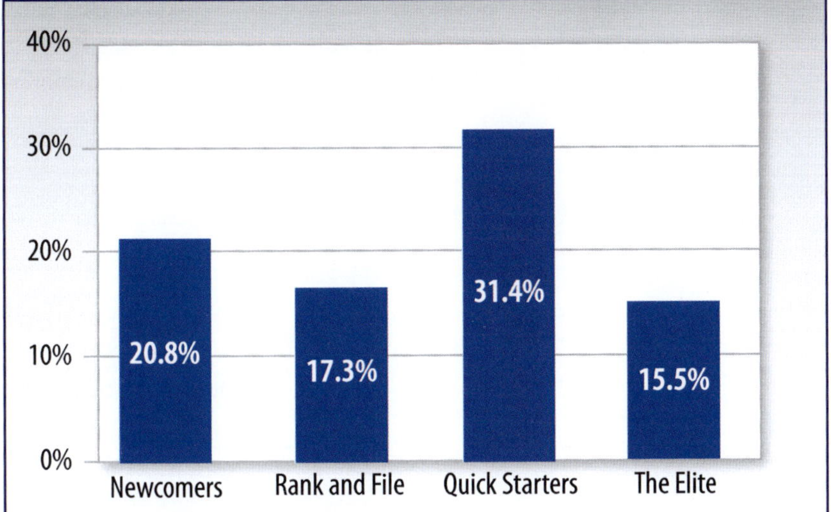

N = 2,103 financial advisors. Source: CEG Worldwide, 2012.

Years of Experience

We already know that both the Newcomers and the Quick Starters have less than five years of experience as financial advisors. But what of the other two groups? Do years of experience explain the difference in the levels of success between the Rank and File and The Elite?

Exhibit 5 suggests that it does not. Although the Rank and File advisors do tend to have less experience overall than The Elite, they still cannot be called an inexperienced group. Notably, nearly one-quarter of the Rank and File (22.7 percent) have been practicing for two decades or more.

EXHIBIT 5
Years of Experience of the Rank and File and The Elite

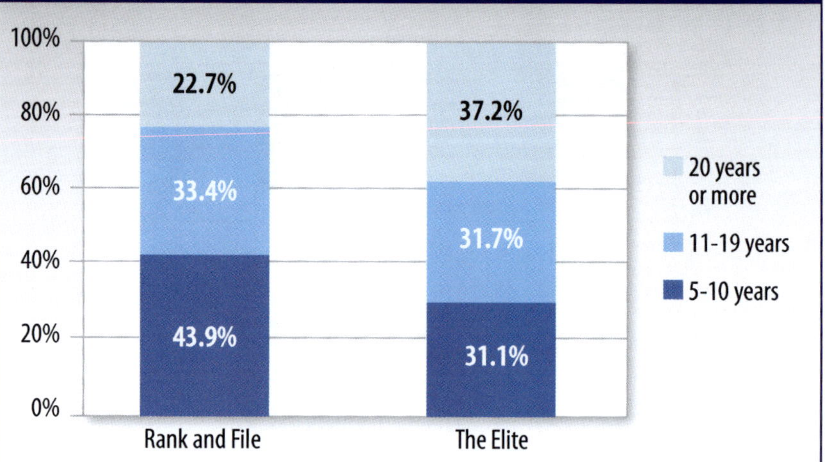

N = 1,527 financial advisors. Source: CEG Worldwide, 2012.

Self-Description

We turn next to the ways in which our respondents describe themselves, an important part of their positioning of their offer and client service. The Quick Starters were the least likely to call themselves "financial advisors"—fewer than half (45.7 percent) use that relatively generic term, compared to nearly two-thirds of the Newcomers (65.1 percent) and half of The Elite (51.2 percent). (See **Exhibit 6.**)

About two in five Quick Starters use either "financial planner" (19.4 percent) or "wealth manager" (18.5 percent), with the remainder split between "investment advisor" and "other." (Terms used in the "other" category include investment expert, technical specialist, personal CFO and life coach.)

We know from prior industry research and our own direct experience that affluent individuals are most interested in working with financial advisors

EXHIBIT 6
How Financial Advisors Describe Themselves

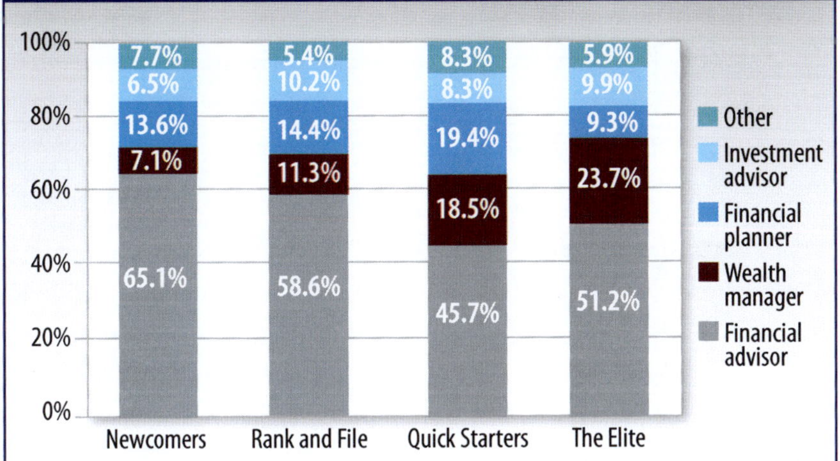

N = 2,128 financial advisors. Source: CEG Worldwide, 2012.

who provide a comprehensive wealth management experience. They are looking for not just investment guidance, but also assistance in addressing their entire scope of financial concerns, including issues in the areas of tax mitigation, estate planning, wealth protection and charitable giving. The financial advisors who can provide this type of wealth management experience have the greatest potential to attract and retain affluent clients over the long run.

Obviously, financial advisors do not become wealth managers simply by calling themselves such. However, positioning as a wealth manager is a necessary first step for effectively attracting affluent clients. As our research shows, financial advisors in The Elite quadrant are most likely to do so, followed by the Quick Starters.

Practice Size

Financial advisors in The Elite group are most likely to have very large practices, with nearly four out of ten (39.7 percent) serving 300 or more

EXHIBIT 7
Number of Clients (Households) Served

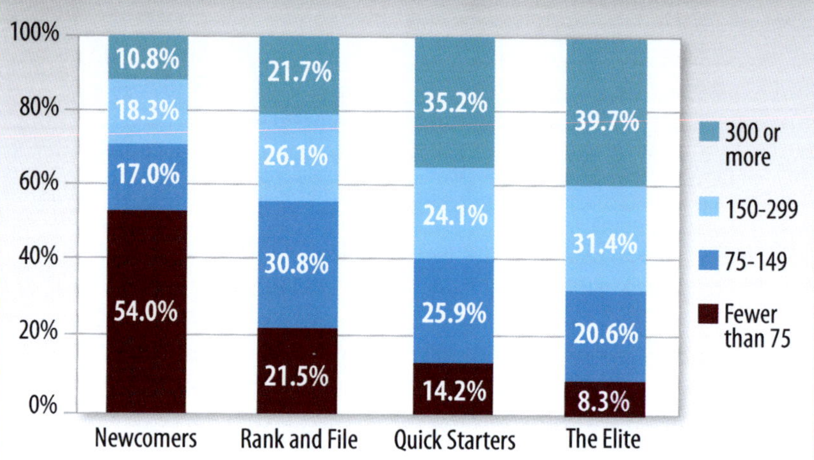

N = 2,128 financial advisors. Source: CEG Worldwide, 2012.

clients. The Newcomers are most likely to serve the fewest clients. Among them, more than half, or 54.0 percent, serve fewer than 75 clients. (See **Exhibit** 7.)

Number of Large Clients

More important to us than the sheer number of clients is the number of clients who are most profitable—those with $1 million or more in assets. In this the Quick Starters and Elites stand far above the Newcomers and Rank and File. As **Exhibit 8** shows, a large portion of both The Elite (39.4 percent) and the Quick Starters (36.1 percent) serve 30 or more of these clients, something that only 2.5 percent of the Rank and File and 1.0 percent of the Newcomers can boast doing.

By drilling down further into these particular data, we can see which financial advisors have practices with a large number of affluent clients—75 or more. **Exhibit 9** shows us that the Quick Starters stand somewhat

EXHIBIT 8

Number of Clients (Households) with at Least $1 Million in AUM

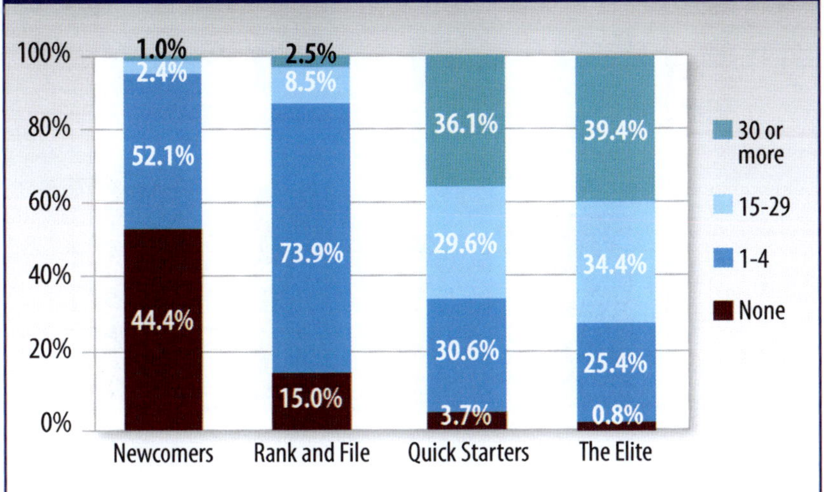

N = 2,128 financial advisors. Source: CEG Worldwide, 2012.

ahead of The Elite in this critical measure. While 22.2 percent of the Quick Starters have built practices that serve a large number of clients with at least $1 million in assets, 15.8 percent of The Elite have done so.

Assets Under Management

By definition, all the Newcomers and Rank and File manage less than $50 million in assets. Among the Quick Starters and The Elite, one might expect that those in business longer—The Elite—would manage more assets, but as **Exhibit 10** shows, this is not the case.

Among the Quick Starters, 13.9 percent are in the extraordinary territory of $500 million or more in assets, compared to 5.4 percent of The Elite. Likewise, more than a quarter of Quick Starters (26.9 percent) have between $200 million and $500 million in AUM, compared to only 17.2 percent of The Elite.

EXHIBIT 9

75 or More Clients (Households) with at Least $1 Million in AUM

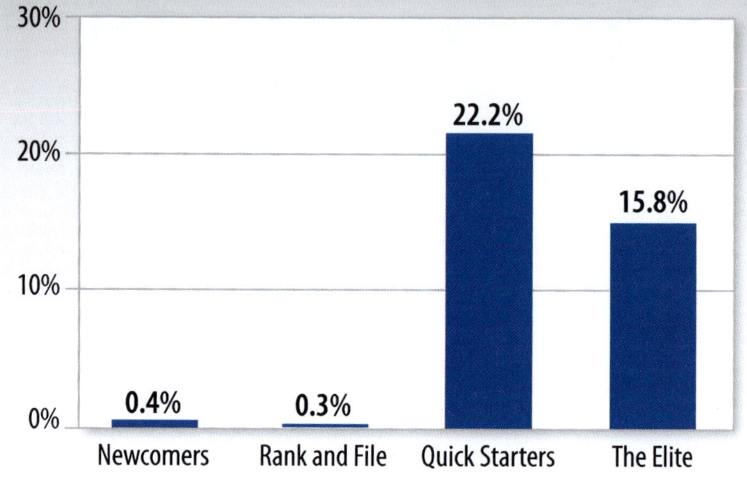

N = 2,128 financial advisors. Source: CEG Worldwide, 2012.

EXHIBIT 10

Assets Under Management of Quick Starters and The Elite

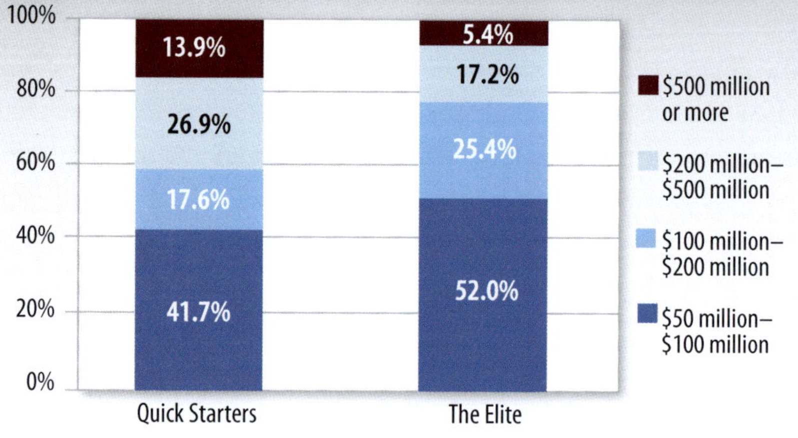

N = 956 financial advisors. Source: CEG Worldwide, 2012.

So despite their brief tenure in the industry, the Quick Starters have managed to accumulate more assets than advisors from every other group. We surmise that, in part, their higher asset levels are due to the success of many Quick Starters in attracting large numbers of $1 million-plus clients, as we saw in **Exhibit 9**.

Net Income

Despite managing more assets than The Elite, the Quick Starters as a whole report far less net income. While two-thirds of Quick Starters (65.4 percent) are earning annual net incomes of less than $100,000, only 13.1 percent of The Elite fall in this lower-income group. And we see a small percentage of Quick Starters in the upper-income ranges: Just 7.7 percent of them earn net incomes higher than $200,000, compared to 49.6 percent of The Elite. (See **Exhibit 11**.)

EXHIBIT 11
Annual Net Income

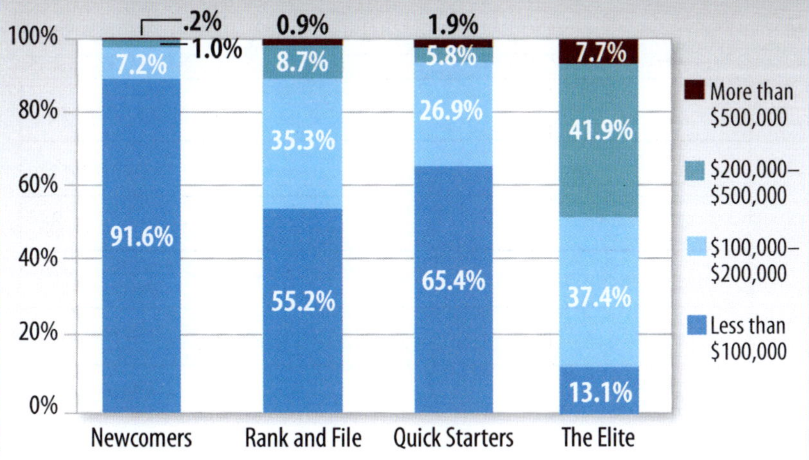

N = 2,097 financial advisors. Source: CEG Worldwide, 2012.

The difference in the net incomes of The Elite and the Quick Starters may be explained by the difference in the stages of their business. The Elite are likely to have scaled and to be well-established, with relatively little need to continue to make major capital investments to expand capacity. The Quick Starters, on the other hand, are likely investing heavily in their businesses, thus greatly reducing their net incomes. These expenses would include hiring new team members, training and developing team members, building the infrastructure of the business (such as office space, equipment, technology, etc.), and expanding their marketing capacity.

Satisfaction with Income

Even though they are bringing home far less net income than The Elite, the Quick Starters' satisfaction with their incomes is nearly as high. (**See Exhibit 12.**) We speculate that because they are choosing to invest substantial revenue into their businesses with an eye on generating significant net income later, they are generally satisfied with their net incomes today.

EXHIBIT 12
Satisfaction with Current Net Income

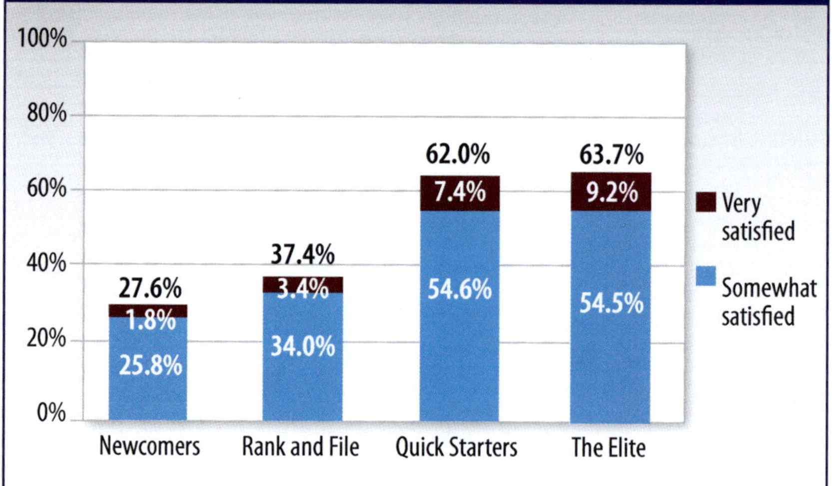

N = 2,128 financial advisors. Source: CEG Worldwide, 2012

We have seen so far that the Quick Starters are experiencing success and satisfaction disproportionate to their experience. From here, we will look at the strategies they are using to achieve their early success, beginning with the heart of every successful financial advisor's business: having the right clients for whom you can add substantial value.

Strategy One: Design the Practice for the Right Clients

Video Overview: www.cegworldwide.com/lead2

AT A TIME WHEN FINANCIAL PRODUCTS AND SERVICES have largely been commoditized, it rarely makes sense for financial advisors to base their value propositions on claims to deliver superior investment returns or unique products. Nonetheless, we see financial advisors attempting to do this every day. For the most part, they are neither satisfying their clients nor growing their net incomes.

We see today's most successful financial advisors having a very different value proposition: the ability to assist clients in making sound decisions about their money—and not just about investments, but about the entire range of their financial challenges—and to do so through satisfying, long-term relationships with their clients.

But you can't provide this type of client service to every individual who walks through your office door. Working only with clients who will be profitable, whom you enjoy and whose needs you can address effectively is an absolute precondition for serving them well.

This calls for designing your business to focus on those clients for whom you can have a huge impact. Here we examine two specific techniques for ensuring that you work with only the right clients.

EXHIBIT 13
Financial Advisors Who Require a Minimum Assest Size to Work with a Client

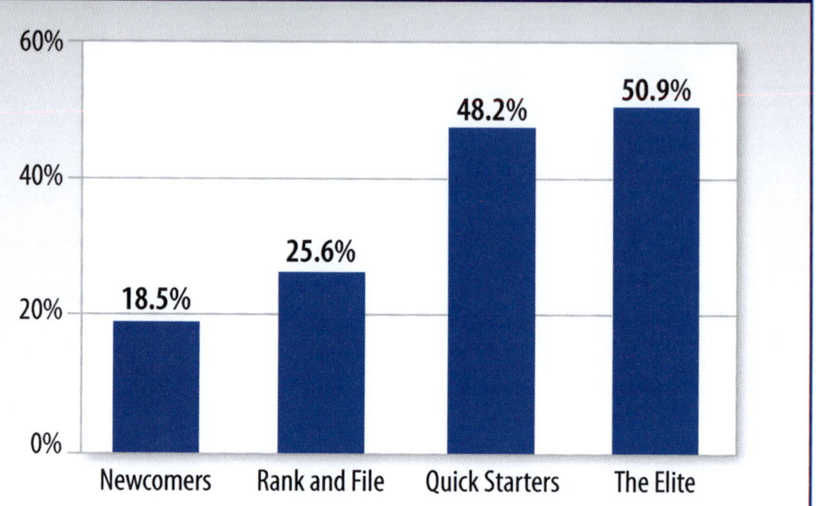

N = 2,128 financial advisors. Source: CEG Worldwide, 2012.

Set a Minimum Asset Requirement

Requiring a minimum account size for new clients is the first step for ensuring that you can serve them profitably. As **Exhibit 13** shows, half of all The Elite (50.9 percent) and nearly half of the Quick Starters (48.2 percent) do so. Among the other groups, the numbers are far lower: Just 25.6 percent of the Rank and File and only 18.5 percent of the Newcomers require a minimum asset size.

Among the financial advisors who do require asset minimums, we see a broad range in the amounts they require. Sizable percentages of both the Quick Starters and The Elite set quite high minimums, with 17.3 percent of the Quick Starters and 16.2 percent of The Elite requiring more than $1 million in assets. The Newcomers and Rank and File who require minimums are far less likely to set the threshold this high: Fewer than 5 percent of each group require at least $1 million in assets, and approximately half of each group set the threshold below $250,000. (See **Exhibit 14**.)

EXHIBIT 14
Required Minimum Asset Levels

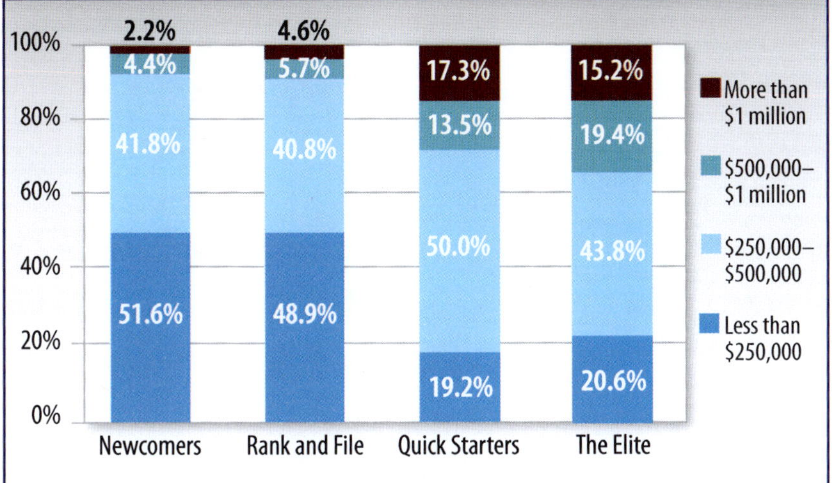

N = 749 financial advisors. Source: CEG Worldwide, 2012.

Some might see the Quick Starters who are setting high minimums despite having relatively little experience as brash. We see them as smart. Not satisfied with marking time, they are taking a deliberate step to focus on the types of clients with whom they can grow very successful practices. And assuming that they have top-notch consultative client service processes in place and access to expertise for addressing clients' advanced financial challenges, there is no reason that those who are newer to the industry cannot serve clients at any asset level extremely well.

Set a Minimum Fee Requirement

Setting a minimum fee for each client or household is closely tied to setting a minimum asset requirement. Doing so ensures that financial advisors are fairly compensated for their work, even when an account drops below

EXHIBIT 15
Financial Advisors Who Require a Minimum Fee to Work with a Client

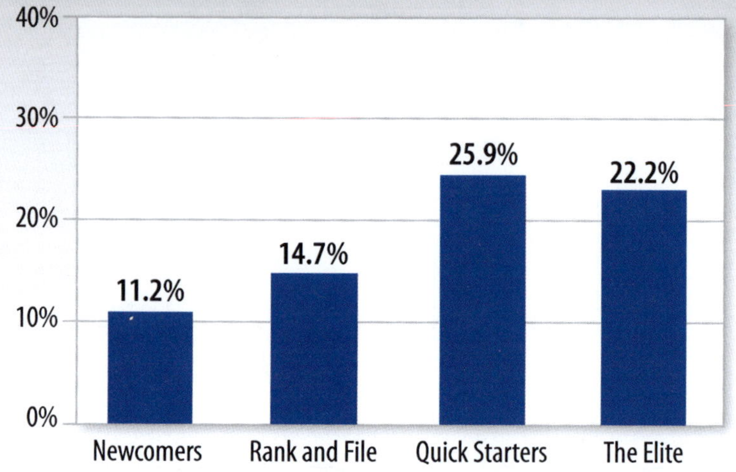

N = 2,128 financial advisors. Source: CEG Worldwide, 2012.

STEPS TO A QUICK START: INSTITUTING A MINIMUM FEE

The following guidelines will help you effectively institute a minimum fee policy in your practice:

1. Once you have decided on the minimum asset level you will require, work backward to set the minimum fee. If we assume that you want to work with clients with assets of at least $1 million and your fee is 1 percent, then your minimum annual management fee for a $1 million client would be $10,000.
2. Should you decide to accept a client with less than $1 million, he or she would still be subject to the minimum $10,000 fee. Keep in mind that the SEC requires that your fee be "reasonable in light of the services rendered," so the account size and the value of your services should be sufficient to make the fee reasonable.
3. Be confident as you institute your minimum fee. Assuming you add real value to your affluent clients' lives, most affluent clients will be quite willing to pay for that value.

a certain minimum. This is particularly important for financial advisors who provide services beyond investment management but are paid only on an asset management fee basis.

As **Exhibit 15** illustrates, financial advisors are less likely to require minimum fees than minimum asset levels, but the percentage requiring a minimum fee stands higher among the Quick Starters (25.9 percent) and The Elite (22.2 percent) than among the Newcomers and Rank and File.

This first strategy has set a foundation for serving the right type of clients: those whom you can serve well and profitably over the long term. It is only a starting point, however. Ensuring that those clients are extremely satisfied is next.

Strategy Two: Serve Clients Extremely Well

Video Overview: www.cegworldwide.com/lead3

IT WOULD BE DIFFICULT TO FIND A FINANCIAL ADVISOR who would not say that it's important to serve your clients well. But the top financial advisors know that good service is not enough. To move to and remain at the highest levels, they must serve the right clients not just well, but extremely well.

World-class client service sets in motion a virtuous cycle that greatly benefits both clients and their financial advisors. When clients are satisfied, they are more likely to remain with their financial advisors over the long term, more likely to provide additional assets to manage and more likely to provide introductions to qualified prospective clients. They are, in other words, more likely to help their financial advisors grow their businesses. This assistance in turn helps free up financial advisors from endless prospecting for new clients, enabling them to focus on continuing to elevate the client experience.

Of course, providing an outstanding client experience requires effort on many fronts. In our discussion of this strategy, we focus on several tactics that we have found to be particularly important for generating high levels of client satisfaction.

Specialize in Serving Specific Types of Clients

As we will see, most financial advisors do not specialize in serving one particular type of client. Because they work with many different kinds of clients, each of whom has different financial goals and challenges, financial advisors must create multiple service models. This time-consuming effort virtually ensures that their clients will not consistently receive a high-quality experience—or if they do, it is only because the financial advisors sacrifice a meaningful profit.

In contrast, when financial advisors focus on a select market of clients with similar needs, they are able to build one streamlined service model and then customize it as needed to meet the specific needs of each client. They realize the benefits of scale while still providing clients the personalized attention they want.

In addition, financial advisors who specialize are able to develop deep expertise in addressing the particular financial challenges of their type of client. Previous industry studies have reported that advisor expertise is

EXHIBIT 16

Financial Advisors Who Specizlize in Serving a Particular Type of Client

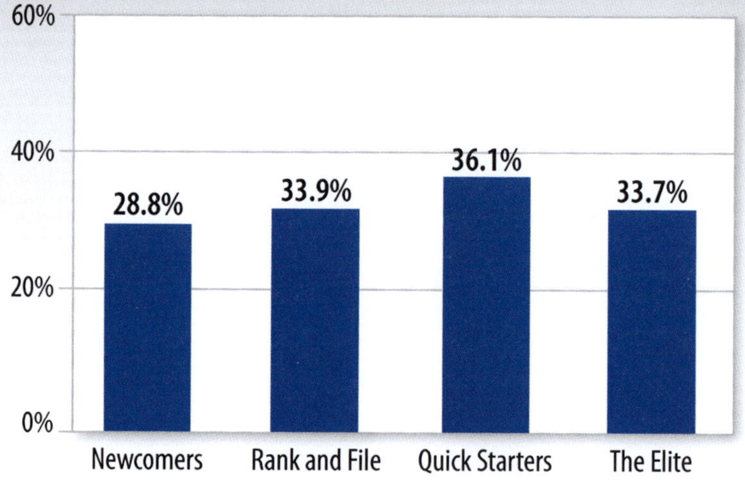

N = 2,128 financial advisors. Source: CEG Worldwide, 2012.

the most important factor for affluent individuals when selecting financial advisors to work with. It is simply not possible to become an expert at solving all types of financial challenges, nor is it credible to claim expertise in all areas. But by specializing in one area, you can go a very long way toward being the expert that your clients need. And where additional expertise is required, you can build a team to provide it.

Which financial advisors are specializing? As we see in **Exhibit 16**, fewer than half of financial advisors from any quadrant serve a particular type of client, though the Quick Starters are slightly ahead of the pack, with 36.1 percent of them focused on serving one type of client.

EXHIBIT 17

Types of Client Specialties

Retirees	46.4%
Private business owners	33.1%
Pre-retirees	31.0%
Family business owners	29.6%
Medical professionals	21.7%
Corporate executives	18.4%
People with inherited wealth	14.3%
Professionals outside of real estate, such as attorneys, architects and accountants	13.8%
Educators	11.3%
Sales professionals	5.3%
Real estate professionals	4.9%
Celebrities	1.4%
Other	19.0%

N = 716 financial advisors. Source: CEG Worldwide, 2012.

Exhibit 17 shows the client types served by the financial advisors who do specialize. Retirees lead the list, constituting a focus of nearly half of the advisors who specialize (46.4 percent). They are followed by private business owners (33.1 percent), pre-retirees (31.0 percent) and family business owners (29.6 percent).

While these areas of specialization are a good start, we believe that they are still too broad. In our work with elite financial advisors in our coaching programs, we have seen the greatest success among those who narrow their focus to very select groups in closely defined geographic areas. These might include, for instance, individuals working in one high-

STEPS TO A QUICK START:
IDENTIFYING WHICH TYPES OF CLIENTS TO SERVE

In our coaching programs, we recommend the following steps to identify the client specialty, or niche, that is best-suited to you and your practice:

1. Identify the largest concentrations of wealth in your area, such as specific communities, industries, companies or professional organizations.
2. Narrow down to three to five promising niches. Each should have a concentration of wealth where you could deliver substantial value to people with whom you would enjoy working.
3. Identify the most significant opportunities. The best means for doing so is to conduct focused interviews with centers of influence in each niche. These will help you better understand the niche and how you could serve it.
4. Analyze your client base to see if you have any clients who belong to any of the niches you are considering. If you do, ask these clients for their perspectives on their communities as well as for introductions to those communities' centers of influence.
5. Choose the one niche that offers the most opportunity yet is narrow enough for you to focus on effectively. The market will quickly tell you whether you have made the right choice.

earning profession (e.g., airline pilots based in Chicago) or who are in a specific circumstance (e.g., retired executives of Lockheed Martin in the Washington, D.C., area).

Exhibit 17 provides some evidence of these types of narrower specialties, including occupations such as medical professionals (21.7 percent), corporate executives (18.4 percent), educators (11.3 percent) and other professionals. Other areas of narrow specialty include people with inherited wealth (14.5 percent) and widows/widowers (14.3 percent).

Leverage a Network of Financial Experts

The tactics we have discussed so far—setting minimum asset and fee requirements and focusing on serving one particular type of client—will go far toward moving you upmarket to serve wealthier clients. But as we know, affluent clients often present complex financial challenges—challenges that may require significant technical expertise.

EXHIBIT 18

Financial Advisors Who Rely on Teams of Experts to Address Clients' Financial Needs

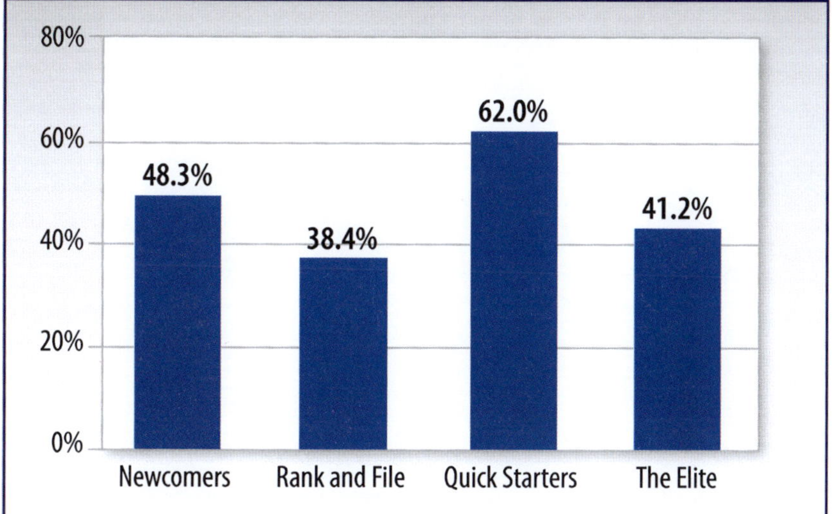

N = 2,128 financial advisors. Source: CEG Worldwide, 2012.

As you specialize in serving one client group, you will surely gain significant expertise in addressing the specific needs of that group. But it is unlikely to be enough. No one person, after all, can be an expert in the fields of estate planning, tax law, asset protection, life insurance, property and casualty insurance, and credit—to name just some of the areas in which the affluent require assistance. To provide the entire range of expertise your affluent clients will require, you must access other professional advisors.

As **Exhibit 18** illustrates, the majority of the Quick Starters understand this, with 62.0 percent reporting that they rely on teams of experts to

STEPS TO A QUICK START:
BUILDING A TEAM OF EXPERTS

You may already have access to an in-house team of experts, particularly if you work with a large firm. If you do not, we recommend creating a team of independent professionals that you can consult on a regular basis. We suggest these steps:

1. Assess your clients' needs to determine the specific expertise they need. We have found that the three professionals most often needed on an expert team are an estate planning attorney, an accountant and a life insurance specialist.
2. Create a list of candidates. Consider resources from financial firms where you already obtain services or products, referrals from clients, and referrals from other financial advisors.
3. Do a bit of research on each candidate to determine his or her potential for adding value to your clients' financial lives.
4. Meet with and interview each candidate. You want to understand the depth of their expertise, how they work with their own clients and how well you might work together on addressing your clients' challenges. Just as important, you want to determine that they work with a high degree of integrity and professionalism.
5. Conduct a test run with the best candidates by inviting them to consult with you and other members of your team on specific client cases. This will help confirm whether you have made the right choice.

address their clients' financial needs. This is critical. As we have seen, the Quick Starters are more likely than all other groups of financial advisors to serve more affluent clients and to manage the most assets. Without reliance on teams of experts, this would be very difficult, if not impossible.

Approximately half of Newcomers (48.3 percent) report working with teams of experts to serve clients. We see this as an encouraging sign that, despite not having large amounts of assets to manage, these financial advisors are seeking to add greater value to their clients. The two groups who have been in the industry the longest—the Rank and File and The Elite—are most likely to stick with the old generalist model, with only about four in ten of each group relying on expert teams to assist their clients.

Be in Close Touch with Clients

World-class client service is predicated on close client contact. Without it, you will not uncover each client's entire scope of financial challenges. You will not hear about changes in clients' lives that mean new financial issues need to be addressed. Nor will you build the rapport that will make your clients stick with you through both good and bad markets.

Just as important, you will miss out on the very real business benefits conferred by close client relationships. Previous research tells us that when clients have regular and meaningful interaction with their financial advisors, those clients are much more inclined both to provide additional assets to manage and to introduce their financial advisors to qualified prospective clients.

Despite this, our study finds that regular client communication is not a priority for a great many financial advisors, especially the less-successful ones. As you will see in Exhibit 19, more than one-quarter of both Newcomers (26.0 percent) and the Rank and File (28.7 percent) contact their best 20 clients, on average, just two or three times or less per year.

The Quick Starters and The Elite are better overall, but many still have room for improvement—in each of those groups, approximately one in six communicates this infrequently with their top clients.

EXHIBIT 19

Frequency of Financial Advisors' Contact with Each Top-20 Client

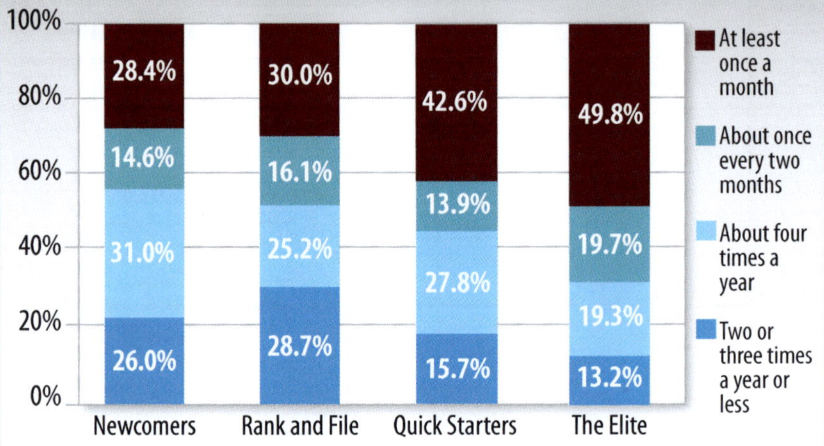

N = 2,128 financial advisors. Source: CEG Worldwide, 2012.

Exhibit 19 also shows us which financial advisors are communicating most frequently. Here The Elite excel, with approximately half, or 49.8 percent, contacting each top-20 client at least once a month. The Quick Starters are not far behind, with 42.6 percent contacting their top clients at least monthly.

As you will recall from **Exhibit 7**, the Quick Starters and The Elite serve the largest numbers of clients on average. Despite this, most still find the time to contact their top clients on a regular basis. We suspect they do so because they understand that client communication is key to client satisfaction—which in turn is crucial to their own success—so they make it a business priority.

STEPS TO A QUICK START:
ENSURING FREQUENT AND MEANINGFUL CLIENT CONTACT

Do not leave effective client communication to chance. Focus on these three actions:

1. Make your contact personal. A client newsletter is not a substitute for a meaningful conversation. Pick up the phone or send a personal email.
2. Make your client contact a systematic part of your everyday work. Leverage your client relationship management technology to prompt regular contact.
3. Make your contact about more than just money. Talk with your clients about other issues that are important to them, such as family issues, sports, hobbies and current events. This type of conversation will build personal relationships much faster than a discussion of last quarter's performance.

Gather Client Feedback

There is a growing recognition among financial advisors that they need their clients' input to deliver the level of service they want. Rather than assuming that they already know how their clients perceive them, they actively solicit their feedback.

As **Exhibit 20** illustrates, the financial advisors most likely to do this are those newest to the industry. Just under two-thirds of the Quick Starters (63.9 percent) and slightly fewer of the Newcomers (61.5 percent) conduct client satisfaction surveys at least once a year. Somewhat less than half of the other two groups do so.

Such surveys send clients a clear message that their financial advisors care about them and their opinions while giving clients permission to point out areas in which their advisors could improve.

EXHIBIT 20

Financial Advisors Who Conduct Client Satisfaction Surveys at Least Annually

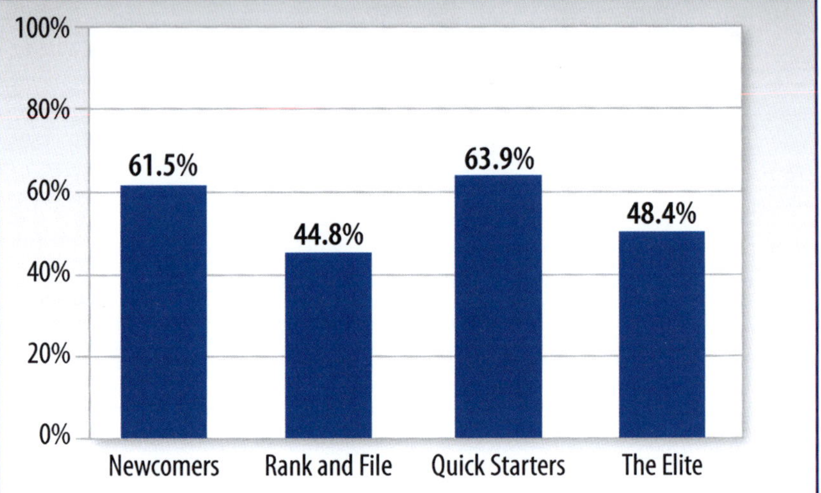

N = 2,128 financial advisors. Source: CEG Worldwide, 2012.

STEPS TO A QUICK START: REQUESTING ADDITIONAL ASSETS

Clients will rarely provide you with additional assets out of the blue. Use these steps to effectively request those assets:

1. Make sure you have a clear understanding of all the assets your clients have and who is managing them. Also be alert to changes in your clients' lives or portfolios that provide openings for a transfer of assets.
2. Frame your request as an offer to conduct a no-obligation diagnostic review of all accounts—those held with you as well as those held at other firms—to determine whether the overall portfolio is properly balanced.
3. When your diagnostic determines that a transfer of assets to your services is appropriate, make that recommendation to the client.

In reviewing this strategy, we have identified the tactics that foster client satisfaction and relationships through outstanding service. Next, we look at how to leverage these relationships to accelerate the growth of the business.

Strategy Three: Effectively Acquire New Assets and Clients

Video Overview: www.cegworldwide.com/lead4

AS WE HAVE JUST SEEN, AN IMPORTANT ELEMENT IN THE success of many of the Quick Starters and The Elite is their focus on building relationships with their clients and with other professional advisors who can assist their clients.

The payoff for these efforts is not just higher client satisfaction. Strong client and professional relationships also provide valuable avenues for growing the business while enabling financial advisors to maintain and even heighten their client focus. In this strategy, we discuss the specific tactics for taking advantage of these opportunities.

EXHIBIT 21

How Many Clients Financial Advisors Regulary Ask for Additional Assets

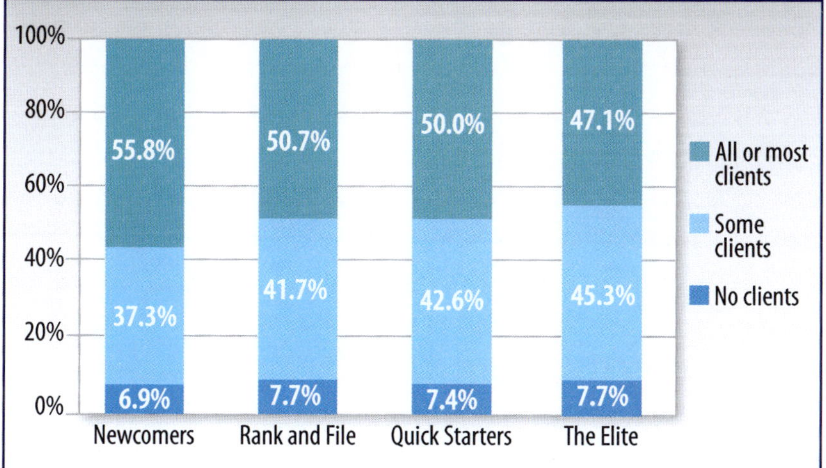

N = 2,128 financial advisors. Source: CEG Worldwide, 2012.

Ask for Additional Assets to Manage

Perhaps the most cost-effective way for financial advisors to increase their assets under management is simply to ask their existing clients for additional assets. Very few financial advisors already manage 100 percent of their clients' assets, so this is fertile ground for nearly everyone.

Exhibit 21 tells us that most financial advisors we surveyed are generally good about this. Those who ask their clients for additional assets on a regular basis range from 47.1 percent of The Elite up to 55.8 percent of the Newcomers. Large proportions of each group regularly ask some of their clients, while few ask no clients at all.

While financial advisors from all groups ask clients for additional assets at similar rates, the results they achieve differ widely. As Exhibit 22 demonstrates, the Newcomers were far more likely to receive smaller amounts. More than half, or 51.4 percent, received less than $50,000 in

EXHIBIT 22

Average Additional Assets Recieved from Each Top-20 Client in Previous Year

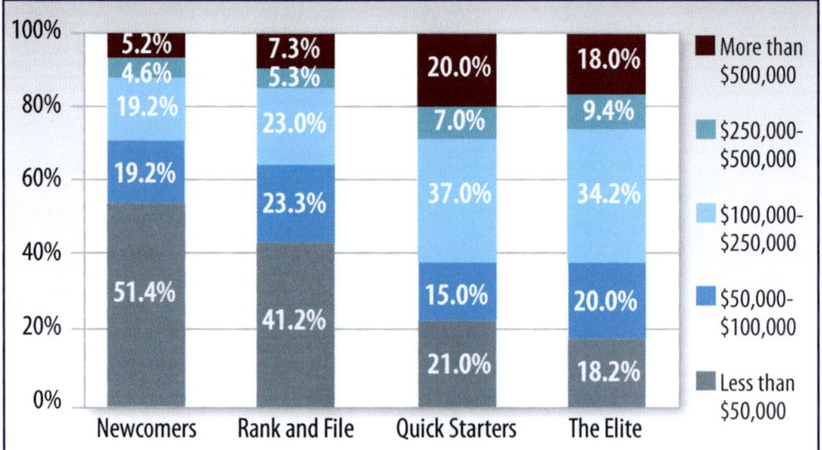

N = 1,970 financial advisors. Source: CEG Worldwide, 2012.

additional assets on average from each of their top 20 clients. This compares to 21.0 percent of the Quick Starters and 18.2 percent of The Elite.

At the other end of the spectrum, a sizable portion of both the Quick Starters and The Elite acquired substantial assets from their top clients, with about one in five advisors in both groups receiving more than $500,000, on average, from each top client. This finding is not surprising—the more-affluent clients of the Quick Starters and The Elite simply have more assets to give—but it does reinforce the value of having those clients in the first place.

Request Introductions to Qualified Prospects

Existing clients are not just an excellent source of additional assets. They also have the potential to assist in bringing in new assets by providing introductions for qualified prospects. This is particularly true for financial advisors who specialize in serving one type of client, as individuals in these groups are often acquainted with one another.

STEPS TO A QUICK START: REQUESTING ADDITIONAL ASSETS

Clients will rarely provide you with additional assets out of the blue. Use these steps to effectively request those assets:

1. Make sure you have a clear understanding of all the assets your clients have and who is managing them. Also be alert to changes in your clients' lives or portfolios that provide openings for a transfer of assets.
2. Frame your request as an offer to conduct a no-obligation diagnostic review of all accounts—those held with you as well as those held at other firms—to determine whether the overall portfolio is properly balanced.
3. When your diagnostic determines that a transfer of assets to your services is appropriate, make that recommendation to the client.

EXHIBIT 23

How Many Clients Financial Advisors Regulary Ask for Referrals

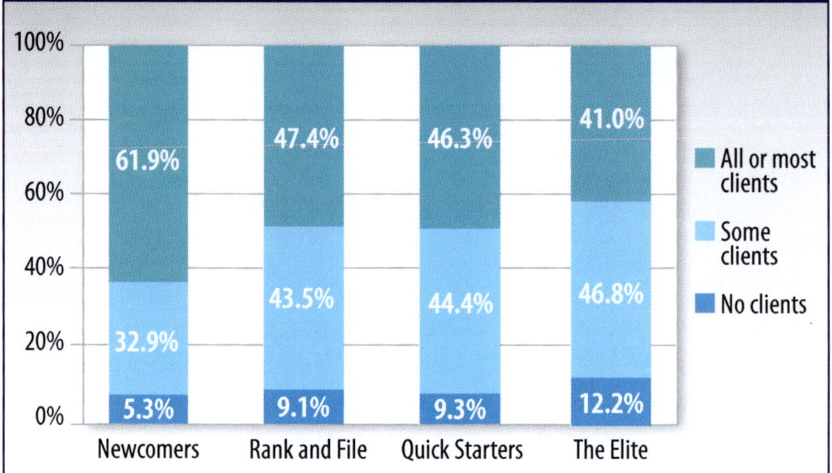

N = 2,128 financial advisors. Source: CEG Worldwide, 2012.

Similar to requesting additional assets, we see from **Exhibit 23** that most of the financial advisors we surveyed regularly ask all or most of their clients for referrals. The Newcomers again excel here, with more than six in ten (61.9 percent) asking all of their clients on a regular basis. While The Elite lag the other groups somewhat, a great majority of this quadrant still requests referrals regularly.

As **Exhibit 24** shows, the majority of advisors who responded to our survey receive referrals from their best clients, although some receive many more than others. Among all groups, around half (ranging from 46.9 percent of the Newcomers to 54.2 percent of The Elite) obtained only one or two referrals, on average, from each of their top clients. In contrast, a relatively small proportion of each group received many referrals (six or more) from each top client. For these financial advisors, client referrals are an extremely productive driver of new business.

EXHIBIT 24
Average Number of Referrals Received from Each Top-20 Client in Previous Year

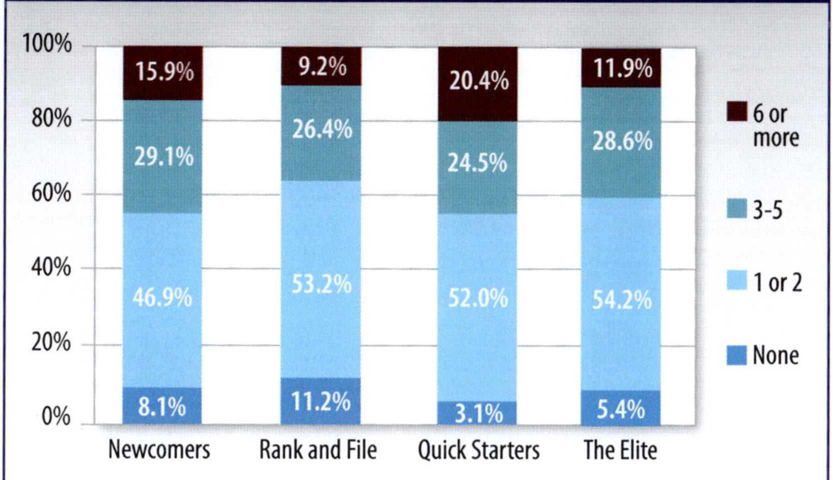

N = 2,128 financial advisors. Source: CEG Worldwide, 2012

Because most advisors ask for referrals regularly, the simple act of asking does not explain the difference between those who receive many referrals and those who receive few. We suspect that the financial advisors obtaining the most referrals have learned how to tailor their referral requests to make them more enticing to their clients. (See the **Steps to a Quick Start** sidebar for our recommendations for effective referral requests.)

Obtain Referrals from Other Professionals

Our final tactic in this strategy—obtaining referrals from other professional advisors—is one that many financial advisors find difficult to implement. Significant numbers of the financial advisors we surveyed receive no referrals at all from other professionals. This ranges from as few as 22.2 percent of the Quick Starters to 46.7 percent of the Newcomers. Half to two-thirds of each group receive these referrals only occasionally. (See **Exhibit 25.**)

STEPS TO A QUICK START:
MAKING A SECOND-OPINION OFFER

Many financial advisors in our coaching programs have experienced considerable success by shifting away from asking for referrals and instead offering to provide a second-opinion service. These are the steps we recommend:

1. Frame your referral request to clients not as a favor to be granted but as an offer to provide a real benefit to the people they care about most. You will deliver this benefit in the form of a complimentary second opinion on the financial situations of the individuals they introduce to you.
2. Ask clients to reach out directly to the people they believe will benefit from your second-opinion service. This personal contact from the client makes the prospective client more inclined to meet with you.
3. Follow up immediately with each prospective client with your offer to conduct a full diagnostic of his or her financial situation.
4. Regardless of how each introduction works out, thank your clients. Acknowledging their assistance will encourage them to provide additional introductions going forward.

This leaves us with small percentages in each group who enjoy a steady stream of referrals. Despite this, from our previous studies we can infer that these referrals are frequently the source of these financial advisors' most qualified prospective clients—and often turn out to be among their best clients.

Why? The professionals who provide these referrals typically know their clients well and are quite familiar with the financial challenges they face. This enables them to refer their clients to financial advisors who specialize in addressing their specific challenges. The resulting matches are beneficial for both clients and advisors.

EXHIBIT 25
How Financial Advisors Describe Their Referrals from Other Professional Advisors

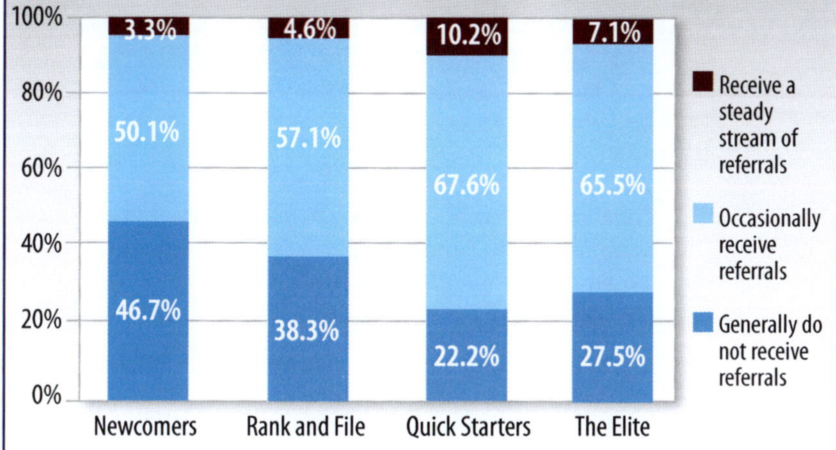

N = 2,128 financial advisors. Source: CEG Worldwide, 2012

EXHIBIT 26
Financial Advisors Receiving Referrals from Professional Advisors

Accountants	61.7%
Attorneys	49.8%
Mortgage brokers	21.3%
Other types of professional advisors	14.3%
Property and casualty insurance agents	12.5%
Life insurance agents	9.0%

N = 2,106 financial advisors. Source: CEG Worldwide, 2012.

STEPS TO A QUICK START:
BUILDING BRIDGES TO OTHER PROFESSIONAL ADVISORS

The most successful relationships with other professional advisors are not casual referral arrangements, but strategic partnerships designed to benefit all parties, beginning with clients. Keep these guidelines in mind as you begin building this type of relationship with other professional advisors:

1. The right candidates will have an entrepreneurial outlook. Like you, they should be looking for opportunities to actively grow their businesses while better serving their clients.
2. The arrangement must offer a compelling value to the other professional's clients. Typically, this will be your ability to address one or more of the specific financial challenges faced by their clients.
3. Your arrangement should also create a vested economic interest in each partner to help the other grow. This agreement should be clearly spelled out and committed to by both parties.

Which types of professional advisors provide referrals most frequently? As **Exhibit 26** shows, accountants are the leading referral source, with 61.7 percent of the financial advisors we surveyed reporting that they had been provided referrals by accountants. Second were attorneys, at 49.8 percent, followed by mortgage brokers, at 21.3 percent.

That accountants and attorneys lead this list is not surprising to us, as we have consistently seen these professionals stand out in their potential to provide quality client introductions, particularly to financial advisors who share their target market.

From here we go to our final strategy: putting the plans in place that will set the business on a deliberate course forward.

Strategy Four: Deliberately Grow the Business

Video Overview: www.cegworldwide.com/lead5

At CEG Worldwide, we are big believers in success on purpose—having a vision for exactly where you want to go and then focusing only on the activities that will bring you closer to achieving your goals. Planning brings this vision and focus together into deliberate, prioritized steps. Without a plan, the chances of substantial success are greatly lowered.

In **Exhibit 27**, we see the extent to which financial advisors in each quadrant have made plans for moving their businesses forward. The Quick

EXHIBIT 27
Types of Plans in Place

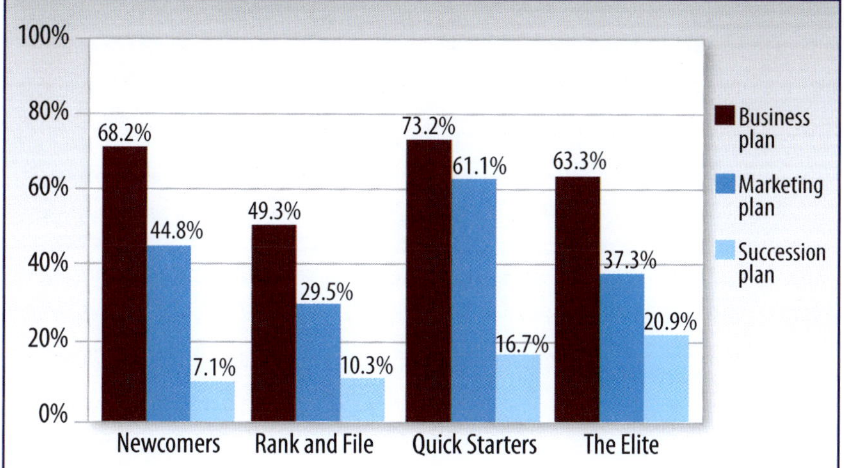

N = 2,128 financial advisors. Source: CEG Worldwide, 2012.

EXHIBIT 28
Financial Advisors Who Have No Type of Plan in Place

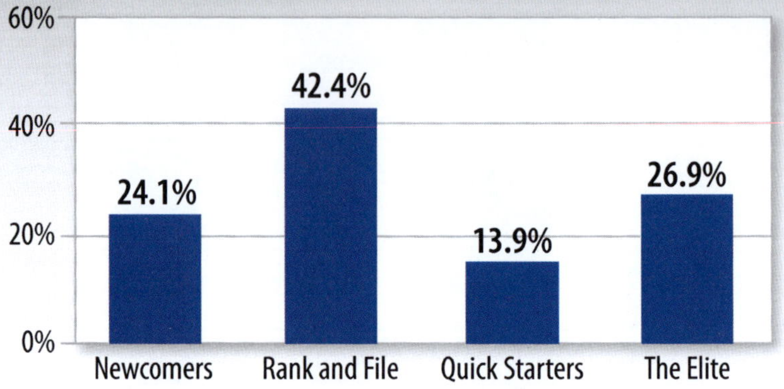

N = 2,128 financial advisors. Source: CEG Worldwide, 2012.

STEPS TO A QUICK START:
EFFECTIVE STRATEGIC PLANNING

The task of business planning can seem so daunting to some financial advisors that they never undertake it at all. Instead of crafting a complex, multipage business plan, we recommend creating a concise, straightforward plan that fits on a single sheet of paper.

1. In just one or two sentences each, describe the primary mission of your business, your most important goals, and your commitment for achieving your mission and goals.
2. Next list the specific actions you commit to taking in the short term, medium term and long term. Define no more than three action items for each time period.
3. Post your plan in a prominent place where you and your team will see it every day.

Starters are most likely to have business plans in place (73.2 percent), while the Rank and File are the least (49.3 percent). The Quick Starters lead in marketing planning as well, with 61.1 percent of them having marketing plans in place, compared to just 29.5 percent of the Rank and File. The Quick Starters fall short only in succession planning, with just 16.7 percent of them having succession plans, compared to 20.9 percent of The Elite.

The level of planning in which financial advisors engage can reveal much about their attitudes toward growing their businesses. Just as revealing is the failure to plan completely. Exhibit 28 tells us that more than four out of ten of the Rank and File (42.4 percent) are adrift without any type of plan at all, despite being in business for at least five years. The same can be said about approximately a quarter of both the Newcomers and The Elite, but only 13.9 percent of the Quick Starters.

Conclusion

Video Overview: www.cegworldwide.com/lead6

WE CONCLUDE WITH ONE FINAL LOOK AT THE RESEARCH, this time into the satisfaction that financial advisors are experiencing overall in their practices. As Exhibit 29 shows, the majority of our surveyed financial advisors report being either somewhat or very satisfied. Among the Quick Starters and The Elite, about five in six report being satisfied, with the Quick Starters slightly edging out their more-experienced peers.

EXHIBIT 29
Satisfaction with Overall Practice

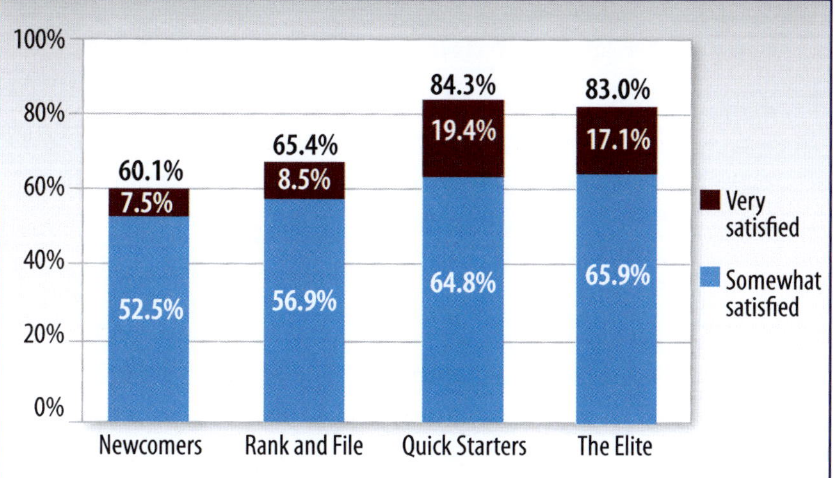

N = 2,128 financial advisors. Source: CEG Worldwide, 2012.

What the Quick Starters are doing is clearly working. In a relatively short amount of time, they have grown their assets under management to the highest levels of all financial advisors and built practices designed to attract and then delight the right clients. As a result, they enjoy the highest overall levels of satisfaction.

And this, ultimately, is what these young financial advisors have to teach us: Time in the industry is not important; deliberate action is. Showing up at work every day does not make financial advisors more successful or their clients more satisfied. Focused effort in a handful of key areas does.

As you continue in your own practice, we encourage you to do so thoughtfully, keeping in mind the actions we have recommended to accelerate your progress and move you closer to your goals while serving your clients well. We wish you the best of success.

An Invitation to Participate in Ongoing Research

To continue helping financial advisors move to higher levels of success, CEG Worldwide conducts research on an ongoing basis through our online panel of more than 1,000 financial advisors nationwide.

If you are a financial advisor who is currently working with clients, we invite you to join our panel. If you choose to do so, we will contact you via email three to four times per year with opportunities to provide your input on a range of issues of interest to financial advisors. To thank you for your participation, we will offer you special reports and results from the panel that will not otherwise be generally available, as well as other bonuses. If you are interested in joining our panel, please visit http://e.cegworldwide.com/panel.

About CEG Worldwide

Video Overview: /www.cegworldwide.com/lead-about

CEG Worldwide is the #1 coaching organization for the financial services industry. We coach financial advisors to achieve breakthrough results in their careers by substantially increasing assets under management, accelerating affluent client acquisition and growing personal net income—all while serving their clients well. We deliver insights garnered from empirical research on industry best practices and coach financial advisors to implement these practices in their businesses. The result: focused, energized and enriched financial advisors who build substantial economic value in their practices, deliver a world-class experience to their clients and ensure a high quality of life for themselves.

CEG Worldwide also works collaboratively with leaders of financial institutions to grow new net assets under management and the loyalty of their top financial advisors while attracting new top financial advisors. We provide insights, developed from empirical research, into what motivates top financial advisors, how to help them stay fully engaged and how to accelerate the achievement of their professional goals. Our services secure the long-term success and allegiance of top financial advisors who generate significant income for financial institutions.

About Meridian-IQ

Meridian-IQ is the premier advisor market database and also represents the next-generation sales and marketing workflow engine incorporating the deepest and most accurate advisor database, time management tools and business planning software.

Meridian-IQ has been developed by a team with decades of combined experience working with hundreds of financial institutions to help them utilize information and tools to most effectively drive their sales, marketing and research efforts in the advisor space.

Meridian-IQ is the first system of its kind to deliver both the data and software tools needed to efficiently maximize business with advisors.

About the Authors

John J. Bowen Jr.

CEO John Bowen founded CEG Worldwide in 2000, with the goal of bringing to bear the lessons he had learned during his career for the benefit of financial advisors and the institutions that work with advisors. His 26 years as a financial advisor and investment firm CEO had taught Bowen that many advisors lacked the high-quality empirical data and pragmatic business experience necessary to build hugely successful businesses. Bowen founded CEG Worldwide to fill that void, with the belief that providing financial advisors and institutions with research about the best practices of elite financial advisors—and the coaching to use these practices effectively—would help them achieve new levels of success while serving their clients extremely well.

CEG Worldwide represents the culmination of Bowen's unique financial services industry experience. That experience encompasses a career as a financial advisor, including eight years as CEO of Reinhardt Werba Bowen Advisory Services, where he was responsible for more than $1.6 billion in assets. Bowen sold that company and subsequently became CEO of Assante Capital Management, where he served as a member of the senior team as the firm more than tripled assets under management to more than $25 billion. Through these experiences, Bowen learned firsthand the best practices for substantial success. He also learned that the vast majority of financial advisors and institutions lacked a road map to build a simple and elegant practice—so he founded CEG Worldwide to provide other financial advisors and institutions the lessons his experience had taught him.

Bowen is widely recognized as a leader in the financial services industry. He writes a highly acclaimed monthly column for the leading U.S. financial services trade journal, *Financial Planning*. He is the author or co-author of several books, including *Breaking Through: Building a World-Class Wealth Management Business, The Prudent Investor's Guide to Beating Wall Street at Its Own Game* and *Creating Equity: How to Build a Hugely Successful Asset Management Business.*

Paul Brunswick

Paul Brunswick brings proven coaching and leadership skills to the CEG Worldwide team. He has extensive financial services experience and a proven track record working with both institutional and ultra-high-net-worth clients, as well as with financial advisors and branch managers. Brunswick has both field and corporate expertise in developing talent at all levels within a financial services organization.

Brunswick has had more than 20 years of success in the financial services industry. Most recently, he was the director of national business development for Smith Barney, where he provided strategic and tactical direction to the firm's entire private client distribution channel. He led campaigns designed to increase financial advisor net asset flow, grow fee-based revenue, and improve financial advisor competency in such key areas as investment and wealth management. He also had responsibility for internal communications, new product approval and the research strategy group.

Earlier, he worked at Smith Barney in a variety of management positions across the country. He started his financial career as a financial consultant for Merrill Lynch in St. Louis, Missouri.

Jonathan J. Powell

Jonathan Powell's considerable expertise in developing top-performing financial advisors is a great asset to the clients he serves through CEG Worldwide. Working with many of the nation's top financial firms, he enjoys helping financial advisors transform their professional and personal lives by using CEG Worldwide's research-backed principles.

Powell has hired and coached hundreds of the industry's top financial advisors—in multiple distribution channels—for more than 25 years. After starting his career as an independent financial planner in the San Francisco Bay area, he went on to spend more than two decades with Citigroup before retiring to pursue his passion for training and coaching.

In his lengthy career, Powell has managed branches for Smith Barney and led Citibank's West Coast brokerage business, overseeing 290 financial advisors and 20 managers. While at Citigroup, Powell was a sought-after speaker for national and regional conferences on topics including time management, financial advisor strategies for success and effective recruiting.

Powell earned a BA in economics from Stanford University and holds the CFP® certification. He is a co-author of *Breaking Through: Building a World-Class Wealth Management Business.*

Printed in Dunstable, United Kingdom

91342915R00033